COLLECTOR'S COMPANION to

CARNIVAL GLASS

SECOND EDITION

IDENTIFICATION
&
VALUES

BILL EDWARDS

MIKE CARWILE

COLLECTOR BOOKS

A Division of Schroeder Publishing Co., Inc.

Front Cover:
Morning Glory funeral vase in blue,
Imperial Glass Co., very rare, $10,000.

Cover design by Beth Summers

Book design by Allan Ramsey

COLLECTOR BOOKS
P.O. Box 3009
Paducah, Kentucky 42002-3009

www.collectorbooks.com

The current values in this book should be used only as a guide. They are
not intended to set prices, which vary from one section of the country to another. Auction prices as well as dealer prices vary greatly and are affected by condition as well as demand. Neither the authors nor the publisher assumes
responsibility for any losses that might be incurred as a result of consulting this
guide.

Searching For A Publisher?

We are always looking for people knowledgeable within their fields. If you
feel that there is a real need for a book on your collectible subject and have a
large comprehensive collection, contact Collector Books.

Dedication

To all the newcomers who have just found the wonder of carnival glass. We've produced this small pocket guide with you in mind and we have tried to show most of the patterns you will find in your early adventure.

Preface

This second edition of the *Collector's Companion* has all new patterns and doesn't repeat any from the first edition; thus, it becomes a companion in fact as well as name.

And while the first edition dealt with primary patterns, this one has many of those but also includes some harder to find items as well as many advertising pieces. We are still showing only American glass but perhaps down the road we will include some foreign patterns.

Once again we are using the abbreviated format with only vital information of pattern name, maker, date of production, reproductions (if any), shapes, colors, and values.

We certainly thank all the collectors who purchased our first edition, especially new collectors, many who have written to us to say they found it a useful book, and we hope they will be just as happy with this edition.

Again, let us say this is just a guide and doesn't establish prices which fluctuate from one area to another. Remember carnival glass has to be graded by the buyer as to condition, rarity, desirability, and quality of iridescence. No price guide can tell you what you should invest in a piece of glass.

Bill Edwards
620 W. 2nd Street
Madison, IN 47250
(812) 265-2940

Mike Carwile
180 Cheyenne Drive
Lynchburg, VA 24502
e-mail: carwile@centralva.net

Contents

Contents

The Basics of Carnival Glass Collecting

First comes color. To tell the true color of a piece of carnival glass, hold the piece to a strong light; the base color you see is the color of the piece. The colors given off by the iridescence have little or nothing to do with the true color of the glass. Many have asked us to provide a color chart to aid beginners, but capturing glass colors on paper is nearly impossible. The best advice we can offer on color is to handle as much of this glass as you can, holding it to the light and observing; soon, colors will come naturally, at least the basic colors.

Next, perhaps we should discuss shapes. Bowls and plates are easy to understand as are pitchers, tumblers, and vases; but even those have variations: bowls can be ruffled, unruffled (shallow unruffled bowls are called ice cream shape), deep, or shallow. Pitchers can be standard, smaller (milk pitcher), taller (tankard), or squat. Tumblers can be standard size, tall (lemonade), or small (juice), even as small as shot glasses. Vases can range from tiny 4" bud vases to monster 22" sizes called funeral vases. Vases may be straight topped, flared, or JIP (jack-in-the-pulpit) shaped with one side down and one side up. In addition there are table sets, consisting of a creamer, a sugar, a covered butter dish, and a spooner (this piece has no lid). There are decanters and stemmed goblets of several sizes; there are rose bowls, evident by the lips being pulled in equally around the top of the piece; candy dishes that have the rims flared out; and nut bowls that have the rim standing straight up. There are banana bowls that are pulled up on two sides, baskets that have handles, bonbons that have handles on opposite sides, and nappies with only one handle. In addition we have berry sets (small and large bowls that are deep and usually come with one large bowl and six small ones), orange bowls (large footed bowls that held fruit), handled mugs, and plates (these are shallow without any bowl effect, coming straight out from the base and no higher from base to rim than 2"). Specialized shapes include candlesticks, hatpins, hatpin holders (footed pieces with the rim turned in to hold hatpins), epergnes (pieces that hold flower lilies), card trays (flattened bonbons or nappies), toothpick holders, cracker and cookie jars with lids, stemmed compotes (or comports as they were originally called), hair receivers, powder jars with lids, as well as many, many novelties that include paperweights, animal novelties, and wall pocket vases. Finally we have punch sets which consist of a punch bowl, standard or base, and matching cups. These are all the general shapes of carnival glass. In addition we have many specialty shapes that include light shades, beads, beaded purses, odd whimsey shapes of all sorts that have been fashioned from standard pieces, pintrays, dresser trays, pickle casters in metal frames, and bride's baskets likewise. The list of shapes is almost endless and the beginner should study these and ask other collectors about odd pieces they can't identify.

Now, let's talk briefly about the iridescence itself. By far the major portion of carnival glass items will be found with a satiny finish that has many colored highlights across the surface, like oil on water; but another very popular finish

The Basics of Carnival Glass Collecting

was developed by the Millersburg Company and used by all other makers in limited amounts. This is called "radium" finish and can be recognized by its shiny, mirror-like lustre on the surface. Often, with radium finish, the exterior of the piece has no iridization and the piece has a light, watery shine. Beyond that, some colors, especially pastels such as white, ice blue, and ice green, have a frosty look. This treatment is always satin, never radium. Finally, there is the addition of the milky edge on treatments that are called opalescent. Added to the marigold finish, this is called "peach opalescent" and with the ice blue, it becomes "aqua opalescent." Other opalescent treatments with carnival glass are blue opalescent, amethyst opalescent, lime green opalescent, ice green opalescent, vaseline opalescent, and red opalescent.

Finally, there are many new color labels that have come about over the last few years. These are mostly shadings of primary or secondary colors; they are often hard to understand and harder to describe. Here are a few: moonstone (opaque glass, not as dense as milk glass); clambroth (pale ginger ale color); black amethyst (nearly black glass iridized); horehound (a shade darker than amber); Persian blue (opaque, like moonstone but blue); smoke (grayish, with blue and gold highlights); teal (a mixture of blue and green); vaseline (a mixture of green and yellow); lavender (a pale amethyst); and lime (green with a yellow mix). Lastly, there are a handful of colors, now in vogue, that nobody seems to agree on a definition: things like Renniger blue, a tealish, sapphirey blue, according to some! Have we carried all this too far? Of course, but it isn't in our hands to stop this proliferation of colors. we can only hope the above information proves helpful in some way. Remember, we are all learning and knowledge comes in time and with patience. The trip is worth the effort.

Old Trademarks

Over the years we've had many requests for information about carnival glass trademarks and while this section will be old news to seasoned collectors, it may just help beginners avoid costly purchases they will regret. If it saves just one from mistaking reproductions for old carnival, the effort is well worth it.

Northwood, Imperial, Cambridge, Dugan-Diamond, McKee, Higbee, Jeannette, Sowerby (England), and Cristales de Mexico (Mexico) are the trademarks on old glass that collectors will see. All these companies marked at least a part of their production. The dates for marking vary and range from 1904 to 1939, depending on the company's lifespan and when it first started marking glass.

On the other hand, many well-known glassmakers never marked old glass. These include Fenton, Millersburg, U.S. Glass, Fostoria, Indiana, and others. Fostoria and Fenton used paper labels on their products and over the years these have been washed off. Others depended on advertising to identify their products and marked the packaging.

Now let's take a look at the most often seen old glass markings:

Northwood   *Cristales de Mexico*   *Higbee*

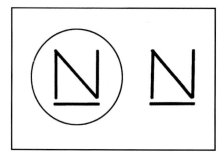

Imperial

Diamond
(Dugan-Diamond)

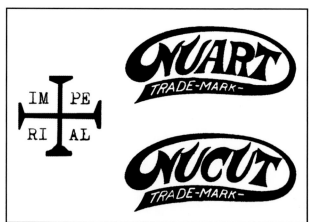

Cambridge

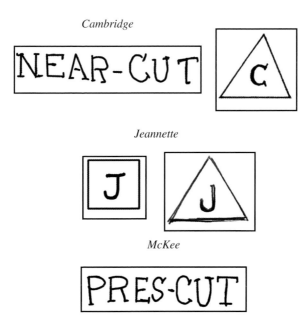

Jeannette

McKee

New Marks

New glass trademarks generally fall into two categories: marks intended to appear close enough to old, well-known trademarks to fool buyers, or completely new trademarks that bear no resemblance to old markings. Here are some of each, all familiar to many carnival glass collectors and dealers. Remember, the old Northwood trademark is owned by the American Carnival Glass Association; the purchasing of this trademark was done to keep it from being copied and the hard work of this organization has stopped many dishonest attempts at copying. The A.C.G.A. has to be commended for its efforts, but as you can see from the first two modern markings, clever attempts to deceive weren't completely stopped. Here are the most often found new marks:

L.G. Wright

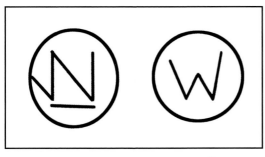

This trademark, often found on many patterns that were made in old carnival, is an obvious attempt to fool the buyer into believing the product is old Northwood and has caused great confusion over the years.

New Marks

Boyd

Boyd is currently using this mark on many types of glass including carnival as well as making some items that are not marked.

Mosser

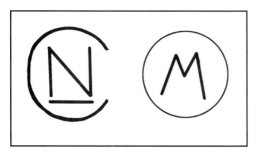

Once again, an attempt to deceive the buyer into thinking the product was Northwood. This mark is even more deceptive than the Wright mark and can be found on Northwood patterns that were also made in old glass. Beware! In addition, Mosser has a third mark, consisting of an "M" inside the outline of the state of Ohio. All three marks can be found on new carnival glass as well as other types of glass.

Fenton

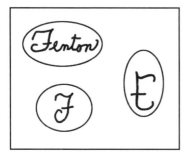

The Fenton Company has been the most responsible glasshouse as far as marking its new glass reproductions. Beginning in 1971 virtually every piece of glass from the Fenton factory has been marked and the company is to be complimented.

Smith Glass Company

Summit Glass Company

Imperial *(1951 – 1972)*	*Imperial Glass* *Liquidation Corp.* *(1973 – 1981)*	*Imperial Glass* *Lorch Ownership* *(1981 – 1982)*

The Imperial Company began using its well-known "IG" mark on reissue patterns in 1951 and marked just about all its products until the company's liquidation in 1973 when a large "L" was added. In 1981 Arthur Lorch bought the company and added an "A" to the trademark. In 1982, Mr. Lorch sold the plant to Robert Stahl who declared bankruptcy in 1984 and closed the factory in 1985. Molds were sold and some were purchased by Summit Glass and are still in production. In addition, Rosso Glass of Pennsylvania reproduces glass in carnival and other treatments and its mark is an "R" in a keystone shape.

Many companies are making new carnival from old molds or creating new molds never found in old glass production. The Indiana Glass Company of Dunkirk, Indiana, has revived some of its old patterns and created new ones. Its large production of geometric patterns in red carnival and the copycat version of the Imperial 474 vase in red have caused unexperienced collectors concern for many months, and hardly a week goes by I don't hear from someone who bought these as old glass. Other small concerns are copying old patterns in carnival and opalescent glass without marking them in any way. So please be cautious; buy only what you know is authentic. If a pattern shape or color not listed in this book shows up in a mall booth, it is probably not old. Toothpick holders, table set pieces, and water set pieces seem to be the most copied shapes but there are bowl copies flooding the stands from the East, especially Taiwan and Hong Kong. Many Northwood, Fenton, and other company patterns are among these, so beware!

About Pricing

Pricing carnival glass is a difficult task because one must take into account not only patterns, colors, and shapes but also the quality of the iridescence. Beginning collectors sometimes fail to understand that a price guide cannot reflect individual sales. At the same time, advanced collectors have complicated the mix by concocting new colors or shades of colors that affect prices.

All prices we list are based on extensive research of auction sales, shop taggings, and private sales where information was forthcoming, and some are pure speculation on pieces that seldom change hands.

Also known as
Diamonds #900

Made by
Diamond Glass Co., 1925

Candleholders, pair, pressed, or blown
Marigold	95
Ice Green	145
Celeste Blue	125

Covered Candy
Marigold	90
Ice Green	120

Fan Vase
Marigold	45
Ice Green	70
Celeste Blue	175

Pitcher
Marigold	160
Ice Green	300
Celeste Blue	425

Tumbler
Marigold	40
Ice Green	60
Celeste Blue	75

Age Herald

Also known as
Birmingham Age Herald

Made by
Fenton, 1911

Bowl, 9", scarce
 Amethyst or Purple   1,300

Plate, 10", scarce
 Amethyst or Purple   2,600

Made by
Dunbar, 1936

Hat Whimsey
Marigold   75

Pitcher, late (either shape)
Marigold   60

Tumbler, late (either shape)
Marigold   10

Vase Whimsey from Pitcher
Marigold   100

Banded Drape

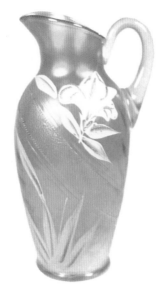

Also known as
Ribbon and Drape, Iris and Ribbon

Made by
Fenton, 1912

Pitcher
Marigold	200
Green	500
Blue	400

Tumbler
Marigold	40
Green	75
Blue	50

Made by
Northwood, 1910

Bonbon (scarce, stippled, add 25%)

Marigold	300
Amethyst or Purple	400
Blue	465
Vaseline	300

Beaded Basket

Made by
Diamond, 1915 – 1916

Basket, flared
Marigold	25
Amethyst or Purple	225
Green	275
Blue	300
White	125
Aqua	400

Basket, straight sided
Amethyst or Purple	350

Also known as
Beaded Medallion and Teardrop

Made by
Imperial, 1912

Vase 8" – 14"
Marigold	65
Amethyst or Purple	235
Green	200
Amber	225

Vase, squat, 5½" – 7½"
Marigold	85
Amethyst or Purple	300
Green	185

Vase, mold proof, scarce
Marigold	125

Beaded Shell

Also known as
Shell, New York

Made by
Dugan, 1910

Reproductions
yes

Bowl, footed, 5"
Marigold 35
Amethyst or Purple 40

Bowl, footed, 9"
Marigold 75
Amethyst or Purple 95

Covered Butter
Marigold 130
Amethyst or Purple 150

Covered Sugar
Marigold 90
Amethyst or Purple 110

Creamer or Spooner
Marigold 75
Amethyst or Purple 90

Mug
Marigold 145
Amethyst or Purple 80
Blue 175
Lavender 175

Mug Whimsey
Amethyst or Purple 450
White 700

Pitcher
Marigold 500
Amethyst or Purple 650

Tumbler
Marigold 60
Amethyst or Purple 70
Blue 180

Made by
Fenton, 1905

Banana Boat
Marigold   35

Bowl
Marigold   30

Plate, 9"
Marigold   110

Rose Bowl
Marigold   50

Beauty Bud Vase

Made by
Diamond, 1918 – 1931

Tall Vase, no twigs
    Marigold   20
    Amethyst or Purple   75

Also known as
Fuchsia

Made by
Fenton, 1912 – 1914

Compote, handled, rare

Marigold	2,200
Blue	2,000

Bells and Beads

Made by
Dugan, 1910

Bowl, 7½"
Marigold 45
Amethyst or Purple 90
Green 115
Blue 120
Peach Opalescent 90

Compote
Marigold 70
Amethyst or Purple 75

Gravy Boat, handled
Marigold 55
Amethyst or Purple 70
Peach Opalescent 140

Hat Shape
Marigold 40
Amethyst or Purple 60

Nappy
Marigold 60
Amethyst or Purple 95
Peach Opalescent 100

Plate, 8"
Amethyst or Purple 170

Made by
Unknown, 1909 – 1914?

Vase, 10¼"
Green	4,200
White	3,800
Iridized Milk Glass	4,000

Bird With Grapes

Also known as
Cockatoo

Made by
Unknown, 1916 – 1918

Wall Vase
    Marigold   125

Blackberry (Northwood)

Made by
Northwood, 1912 – 1913

Compote, either exterior pattern
Marigold	85
Amethyst or Purple	100
Green	150
Blue	325
White	150

Blackberry Block

Also known as
Blackberry and Checkerboard

Made by
Fenton, 1910

Pitcher

Marigold	400
Amethyst or Purple	1,250
Green	1,400
Blue	1,250
Vaseline	6,500

Tumbler

Marigold	65
Amethyst or Purple	80
Green	95
Blue	75
Vaseline	350

Also known as
Fenton's #303

Made by
Fenton, 1910

Compote

Marigold	40
Amethyst or Purple	50
Green	70
Blue	55

Blackberry Rays

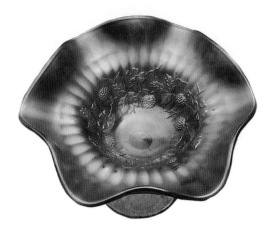

Made by
Northwood, 1910

Compote
Marigold	425
Amethyst or Purple	450
Green	500

Also known as
#1216

Made by
Fenton, 1908

Bonbon
Marigold	35
Amethyst or Purple	45
Green	50
Blue	45
Amberina	400

Compote
Marigold	40
Amethyst or Purple	50
Green	55
Blue	50

Hat Shape
Marigold	45
Amethyst or Purple	100
Green	200
Blue	40
Aqua Opalescent	800
Red	400
Aqua	125

Absentee Variant, J.I.P.
Ice Green	55
White	45

Blossomtime

Also known as
Northwood's Primrose

Made by
Northwood, 1909

Compote
Marigold	275
Amethyst or Purple	325
Green	425

Made by
Unknown, 1920s

Tumbler, rare
Marigold   300

Boggy Bayou

Made by
Fenton, 1912

Vase, 6" – 11"
Marigold	40
Amethyst or Purple	125
Green	150
Blue	135
Vaseline Opalescent	1,450

Vase, 12" – 15"
Marigold	60
Amethyst or Purple	145
Green	160
Blue	150

Made by
Dugan, 1911

Bowl, flat, 8½"
Amethyst or Purple   125
Peach Opalescent   180

Bowl, footed, 8½"
Marigold   175
Amethyst or Purple   475
Peach Opalescent   250

Handgrip Plate
Marigold   350
Amethyst or Purple   495
Peach Opalescent   350

Rose Bowl, scarce
Amethyst or Purple   700
Peach Opalescent   525

Brazier's Candies

Made by
Fenton, 1912

Bowl
Amethyst or Purple   675

Plate, handgrip
Amethyst or Purple   1,000

Made by
Northwood, 1911

Plate, advertising
Amethyst or Purple 3,000

Broken Arches

Made by
Imperial, 1911

Bowl, 8½" – 10"
Marigold   45
Amethyst or Purple   50
Green   75

Punch Bowl and Base, round top
Marigold   400
Amethyst or Purple 1,100

Punch Cup
Marigold   20
Amethyst or Purple   45

**Punch Bowl and Base, ruffled top
and ringed interior pattern, rare**
Amethyst or Purple   2,000

Made by
Diamond, 1930 – 1931

Bowl, scarce
Marigold   325

Bowl, unlettered, rare
Marigold   4,700

Bull's Eye and Loop (Millersburg)

Made by
Millersburg, 1911

Vase, 7" – 11", rare
Marigold	600
Amethyst or Purple	500
Green	400

Also known as
Big Butterfly

Made by
U.S. Glass, 1890s (crystal), 1915 (carnival)

Tumbler, rare

Marigold	6,500
Green	10,000

Butterfly and Fern

Also known as
Butterfly and Plume

Made by
Fenton, 1911

Pitcher

Marigold	325
Amethyst or Purple	400
Green	650
Blue	425

Tumbler

Marigold	45
Amethyst or Purple	55
Green	85
Blue	65

Variant Pitcher (no ferns), rare

Marigold	3,000

Also known as
#2699

Made by
Cambridge, 1913

Reproductions
yes (crystal)

Cruet, 4", scarce
Green   575

Cruet, 4", with metal tag,
B.P.O.E.#1, rare
Green   1,000

Cruet, 6", scarce
Marigold   425
Green   400

Buzz Saw and File

Made by
Unknown, 1914 – 1916

Goblet
    Marigold   175

Pitcher
    Marigold   350

Tumbler, juice
    Marigold   150

Tumbler, lemonade
    Marigold   175

Also known as
#2660/108

Made by
Cambridge, 1914 – 1916

Cologne bottle, one size, very scarce
Marigold   600
Green   850

Cameo Medallion

Made by
Westmoreland, 1909 – 1912

Basket, three sizes
Marigold   35 – 75

Campbell and Beesley

Also known as
Spring Opening

Made by
Millersburg, 1911

Plate, advertising, handgrip
Amethyst or Purple   1,400

Canada Dry

Also known as
Sparkling Orangeade

Made by
Unknown, 1923

Bottle, two sizes
    Marigold   25
    White   45
*Double price for unopened with all labels

Tumbler Whimsey, cut from bottle
    Marigold   45

Also known as
Flute and Cane

Made by
Imperial, 1915

Bowl, 7½" – 10"
Marigold   30 – 35

Bowl Square Whimsey
Marigold   70

Champagne, rare
Marigold   150

Compote, Large
Marigold   60

Milk Pitcher
Marigold   210

Pickle Dish
Marigold   25

Punch Cup
Marigold   25

Pitcher, stemmed, rare
Marigold   400

Tumbler, rare
Marigold   500

Wine
Marigold   60

49

Caroline

Made by
Dugan, 1907 (opalescent), 1910 (carnival)

Bowl, 7" – 10"
Marigold	70
Peach Opalescent	100

Banana Bowl
Peach Opalescent	125

Basket, scarce
Peach Opalescent	250
Lavender Opalescent	600

Made by
Fenton, 1911

Bowl, 6" – 7"
    Amethyst or Purple 1,000

Plate, scarce
    Amethyst or Purple 2,500

Plate, handgrip
    Amethyst or Purple 1,200

Chain and Star

Made by
Fostoria, 1914 – 1917?

Covered Butter, rare
Marigold   1,500

Creamer or Sugar
Marigold   175

Tumbler, rare
Marigold   900

Also known as
#407½

Made by
Imperial, 1909 – 1911

Pitcher, very scarce
    Amethyst or Purple   3,000

Tumbler, very scarce
    Amethyst or Purple   300

Checkerboard

Also known as
Old Quilt

Made by
Westmoreland, 1915

Reproductions
yes

Cruet, rare
    Clambroth   750

Goblet, rare
    Marigold   350
    Amethyst or Purple   250

Punch Cup, scarce
    Marigold   80

Pitcher, rare
    Amethyst or Purple   3,000

Tumbler, rare
    Marigold   675
    Amethyst or Purple   400

Wine, rare
    Marigold   300

Vase, scarce
    Amethyst or Purple   2,400

Made by
Hazel-Atlas, 1920s

Ashtray
  Marigold   40

Bowl, 4"
  Marigold   25

Bowl, 9"
  Marigold   35

Butter, two sizes
  Marigold   200

Plate, 7"
  Marigold   75

Rose Bowl
  Marigold   85

Cherry and Cable

Also known as
Cherry and Thumbprint

Made by
Northwood, 1908

Reproductions
yes

Bowl, 5", scarce
   Marigold   75

Bowl, 9", scarce
   Marigold   110

Butter, scarce
   Marigold   400

Pitcher, scarce
   Marigold   1,200

Tumbler, scarce
   Marigold   150

Sugar, Creamer, Spooner, each, scarce
   Marigold   175
   Blue   350

Made by
Fenton, 1914

Reproductions
yes

Bonbon

Marigold	50
Amethyst or Purple	60
Green	65
Blue	60

Bowl, small, 6" – 6½"

Marigold	25
Amethyst or Purple	60
Green	75
Blue	50

Bowl, 9" – 10"

Marigold	70
Amethyst or Purple	350
Green	300
Blue	85
White	100
Red	6,500
Vaseline	150

Plate, 6"

Marigold	115
Amethyst or Purple	900
Green	1,350
Blue	175
White	225

Chop Plate, rare

Marigold	2,100
White	1,300

Cherry Smash

Also known as
Cherryberry

Made by
U.S. Glass, 1929 – 1931

Reproductions
yes

Bowl, 8"
   Marigold   55

Butter
   Marigold   160

Compote, 3¾", scarce
   Marigold   75

Pitcher, very scarce
   Marigold   225

Tumbler
   Marigold   150

Chesterfield

Also known as
Imperial #600

Made by
Imperial, 1914 – 1916

Champagne, 5½"
Marigold 35
Red 175
Smoke 50

Candlesticks, pair
Marigold 60
Smoke 105

Compote, 6½"
Marigold 35
Clambroth 40

Compote, 11½"
Marigold 75
White 95
Red 400
Smoke 125

Candy with lid, tall
Marigold 65
Red 300
Smoke 90

Pitcher with lid
Marigold 150
White 300
Red 600

Tumbler
Marigold 35
White 70
Red 250

Punch Bowl and Base
Marigold 500

Punch Cup
Marigold 50

Rose Bowl
Marigold 45
Smoke 60

Lemonade Mug, handled
Marigold 50
Clambroth 40

Sherbet, two sizes
Marigold 25
Red 80
Teal 50

Table Salt
Marigold 85
Clambroth 60

Toothpick, handled
(add 25% for Iron Cross)
Marigold 250

59

Christmas Compote

Made by
Dugan, 1913

Reproductions
yes

Large Compote, scarce
Marigold   5,500
Amethyst or Purple   4,000

Made by
Dugan, 1907 (opalescent), 1910 (carnival)

Bowl, 5"
Marigold	40
Amethyst or Purple	45

Bowl, 10"
Marigold	65
Amethyst or Purple	80

Butter or Sugar
Marigold	375
Amethyst or Purple	425

Compote, scarce
Amethyst or Purple	225

Creamer or Spooner
Marigold	95
Amethyst or Purple	175

Hat Shape, scarce
Marigold	60
Amethyst or Purple	95

Pitcher, rare
Marigold	1,600
Amethyst or Purple	2,200

Tumbler, very scarce
Marigold	350
Amethyst or Purple	425

Vase Whimsey, scarce
Marigold	135
Amethyst or Purple	265
Black Amethyst	300

Cleveland Memorial

Made by
Millersburg, 1911

Ashtray, rare
Marigold   15,000
Amethyst or Purple 7,000

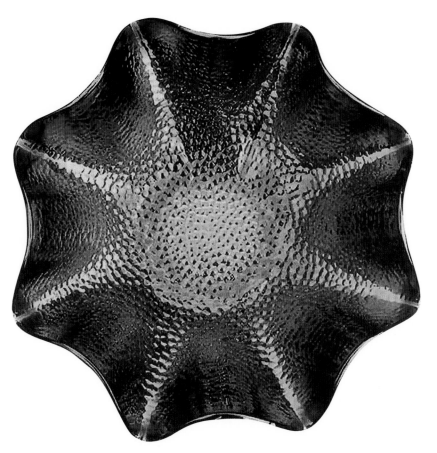

Also known as
Bubbles and Peacock Eye

Made by
Imperial, 1913

Bowl, 8½"

Marigold	135
Amethyst or Purple	300
Green	125
Blue	500
Amber	275

Plate, rare

Amethyst or Purple	1,300

Coin Dot

Made by
Fenton, 1917

Bowl, 6" – 10"
Marigold	30
Amethyst or Purple	50
Green	50
Blue	45
Aqua Opalescent	150
Red	1,100
Lavender	100

Plate, 9", rare
Marigold	200
Blue	260

Rose Bowl
Marigold	100
Amethyst or Purple	150
Green	175
Blue	140
Red	1,450

Made by
Imperial, 1916

Vase, scarce
    Marigold   1,000
    Amethyst or Purple   750

Columbia

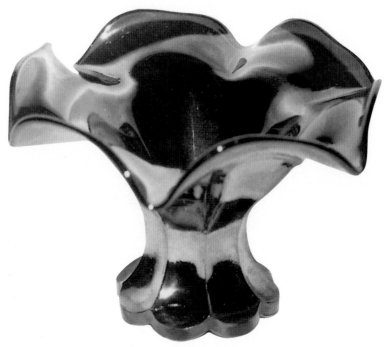

Also known as
Imperial's #246

Made by
Imperial, 1910

Cake Plate, scarce
Marigold	100
Clambroth	75

Compote
Marigold	60
Amethyst or Purple	300
Green	225
Smoke	100

Rose Bowl, rare
Marigold	200

Vase
Marigold	45
Amethyst or Purple	125
Green	165
Smoke	125

Also known as
Latticed Grape

Made by
Fenton, 1911

Bowl, 9"

Marigold	225
Amethyst or Purple	275
Green	550
Blue	300
Amber	400

Plate, 10", rare

Marigold	1,900
Amethyst or Purple	2,400
Green	4,900
Amber	3,500

Cone and Tie

Made by
Imperial, 1909 – 1910

Tumbler, very rare
Amethyst or Purple   3,500

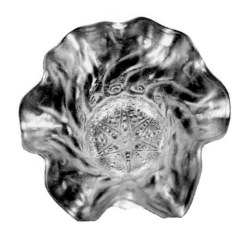

Also known as
Beaded Star and Snail

Made by
Dugan, 1907 – 1912

Compote

Marigold	85
Amethyst or Purple	450
Peach Opalescent	400
White	100
Lavender	425

Coral

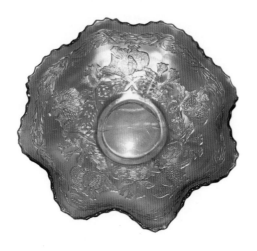

Made by
Fenton, 1915 – 1917

Bowl, 9"

Marigold	325
Green	225
Blue	500
White	400

Plate, 9½"

Marigold	1,350

Also known as
"Ole Corn"

Made by
Imperial, 1913

One Size, scarce
Marigold	375
Green	350
Smoke	400

Corn Vase

Made by
Northwood, 1912 – 1914

Regular Mold

Marigold	1,000
Amethyst or Purple	750
Green	1,000
Blue	2,300
Aqua Opalescent	3,250
Ice Blue	2,500
Ice Green	425
White	400
Lime Green	375

Pulled Husk

Amethyst or Purple	16,500
Green	13,000

Made by
Millersburg, 1910

Bowl, 5", very scarce
Marigold   90

Bowl, 8", very scarce
Marigold   175

Bowl, 10", very scarce
Marigold   295

Bowl, square, very scarce
Marigold   500

Covered Butter, rare
Marigold   650
Amethyst or Purple   900

Creamer or Spooner
Marigold   300
Amethyst or Purple   350
Green   750

Spittoon Whimsey, rare
Amethyst or Purple   4,650

Sugar with Lid
Marigold   325
Amethyst or Purple   400
Green   800
Vaseline   2,000

Vase Whimsey, two sizes, rare
Marigold   850
Amethyst or Purple   1,350

Courthouse

Made by
Millersburg, 1910 – 1911

Bowl, lettered, scarce
    Amethyst or Purple   875
    Lavender   2,800

Bowl, unlettered, rare
    Amethyst or Purple 4,000

Also known as
Blaze

Made by
Imperial, 1909 – 1912

Bowl, 5"

Marigold	25
Amethyst or Purple	35
Green	40
Smoke	65

Bowl, 8" – 10"

Marigold	50
Amethyst or Purple	125
Green	95
Smoke	75

Creole

Made by
Unknown, 1910 – 1914?

Rose Bowl, stemmed
Marigold   750

Made by
Imperial, 1910 – 1914

Reproductions
yes

Candlestick, each, rare
Marigold   600

Cut Cosmos

Made by
Not Confirmed, 1909 – 1912

Tumbler, rare
Marigold   225

Made by
Jenkins, 1914 – 1918

Vase, 10"
    Marigold   125
    Smoke   140

Daisy Cut Bell

Made by
Fenton, 1914

One size, scarce
Marigold   350

Made by
Westmoreland, 1911 – 1913

Celery Vase Whimsey
    Marigold   600

Compote, various shapes, rare
    Marigold   575
    Amber   700

Goblet, rare
    Marigold   600
    Amethyst or Purple 750
    Amber   900

Rose Bowl, scarce
    Marigold   475
    Green   600
    Ice Green   625

Davidson's Society Chocolates

Made by
Northwood, 1912

Plate, handgrip
Amethyst or Purple   1,000

Made by
Millersburg, 1911

Compote, rare
Marigold 1,800
Amethyst or Purple 2,200
Green 2,000
Blue 7,000

Compote, ruffled top, rare
Amethyst or Purple 2,500

Rose Bowl, stemmed, rare
Green 8,000

Diamond and Daisy Cut

Made by
U.S. Glass, 1916 – 1918

Pitcher, rare
Marigold	400
Blue	450

Tumbler, 5", rare
Marigold	150

Tumbler, 4", very scarce
Marigold	65
Blue	95

Vase, square, 10"
Marigold	225

Also known as
Palm Leaf Fan

Made by
Higbee, 1909

Bowl, scarce
Marigold   100

Cruet, very scarce
Marigold   425

Plate, handgrip, rare
Marigold   250

Diamond Points

Made by
Northwood?, 1914 – 1916

Basket, rare
Marigold	1,400
Amethyst or Purple	2,100
Blue	2,500
White	2,800

Made by
U.S. Glass, 1914 – 1916

Tumbler
Marigold   125

Dolphins

Made by
Millersburg, 1911

Compote, rare
 Amethyst or Purple 2,300
 Green   4,000
 Blue   5,700

Also known as
Dolphin Twins

Made by
Fenton, 1909 – 1930s

Reproductions
yes

Bowl, flat, 8" – 10"
Celeste Blue   65

Bowl, footed, 9" – 11"
Celeste Blue   115

Cake Plate, center handle
Celeste Blue   85

Candlesticks, pair
Celeste Blue   90

Compote
Celeste Blue   70

Covered Candy, stemmed
Celeste Blue   80

Fan Vase
Celeste Blue   90

Double Dutch

Made by
Imperial, 1910

Reproductions
yes

Bowl, footed, 9"
Marigold	50
Amethyst or Purple	180
Green	75
Smoke	85

Made by
Fenton, 1914

Bowl, 11", scarce
Marigold   1,200

Shade
Marigold   225
Marigold Milk Glass   150

Dreibus Parfait Sweets

Made by
Northwood, 1909

Plate, two or four sides up
  Amethyst or Purple   850

Plate, flat, rare
  Amethyst or Purple   1,100

Dugan Fancy Husk Corn Vase

Made by
Dugan, 1907 (opalescent), 1910 (carnival)

Reproductions
yes

Fancy Husk, rare
Marigold   1,300

Dugan Smooth Rays

Also known as
Smooth Ribs

Made by
Dugan, 1911

Bowl
Marigold	45
Amethyst or Purple	75
Peach Opalescent	100

Made by
Fenton, 1916 – 1917

**Orange Bowl, footed (Grape &
Cable with advertising), very scarce**
Blue   1,600

E.A. Hudson Furniture

Made by
Northwood, 1912 – 1914

Plate, flat, advertising
Amethyst or Purple 1,700

Bowl, advertising, rare
Amethyst or Purple 1,500

Plate, handgrip, advertising
Amethyst or Purple 1,300

Made by
Unknown (possibly Northwood), 1913 – 1914

Tumbler, enameled, rare
Marigold   350

Pitcher, enameled, rare
Marigold   800

Elks (Dugan)

Made by
Dugan, 1910 – 1914

Nappy, very rare
Amethyst or Purple   7,000

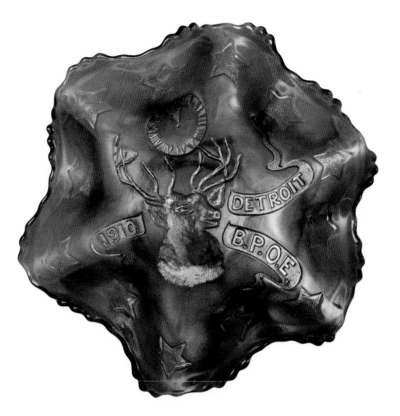

Made by
Fenton, 1910, 1911, 1912, 1914

Detroit Bowl, scarce
Marigold	9,500
Amethyst or Purple	800
Green	1,100
Blue	1,000

Parkersburg Plate, rare
Green	2,000
Blue	2,500

Atlantic City Plate, rare
Green	1,800
Blue	1,800

Atlantic City Bowl, scarce
Blue	1,300

1911 Atlantic City Bell, rare
Blue	2,200

1917 Portland Bell, very rare
Blue	23,000

1914 Parkersburg Bell, rare
Blue	2,500

Elks (Millersburg)

Made by
Millersburg, 1910

Bowl, rare
    Amethyst or Purple 2,500

Paperweight, rare
    Amethyst or Purple 2,500
    Green   4,000

Also known as
Scroll Cable

Made by
Westmoreland, 1909

Bud Vase, 6"

Marigold	50
Smoke	75

Creamer or Sugar

Marigold	55
Peach Opalescent	75
Blue Opalescent	210
Aqua	110

Mug, rare

Marigold	75

Perfume, very scarce

Smoke	400

Fan

Made by
Dugan, 1907

Bowl, sauce, 5"
Marigold	40
Amethyst or Purple	55
Peach Opalescent	100

Gravy Boat, footed
Marigold	65
Amethyst or Purple	180
Peach Opalescent	150

Also known as
Busy Chickens

Made by
Dugan, 1913

Reproductions
yes

Bowl, 10", scarce
Amethyst or Purple	5,000
Green	8,200
Peach Opalescent	11,000

Bowl, 10", square, very scarce
Amethyst or Purple	6,000
Green	10,000

Plate, 10½", very scarce
Amethyst or Purple	18,000

Feathered Arrow

Made by
Unknown, 1915 – 1920

Bowl, 8½" – 9½"
Marigold   65

Rose Bowl, rare
Marigold   200

Also known as
Poplar Tree

Made by
Northwood, 1904 (opalescent), 1912 (carnival)

Vase, 7" – 14"

Marigold	45
Amethyst or Purple	85
Green	75
Ice Blue	200
White	400

Feldman Bros.

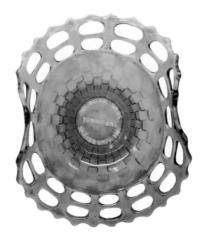

Made by
Fenton, 1910 – 1912

Open Edge Basket
Marigold   65

Also known as
Diamond and Cable

Made by
Fenton, 1910 – 1912

Bowl, footed, 5"
Marigold	30
Amethyst or Purple	70
Green	70
Blue	60

Bowl, footed, 9½"
Marigold	100
Amethyst or Purple	125
Green	125
Blue	110

Butter
Marigold	115
Blue	185

Creamer, Sugar, or Spooner
Marigold	75
Blue	90

Fruit Bowl, 10"
Marigold	85
Blue	100

Pitcher
Marigold	400
Blue	625

Tumbler
Marigold	50
Blue	75

Vase Whimsey, rare
Marigold	325
Blue	450

Fenton's Cherries

Also known as
Cherries and Mums

Made by
Fenton, 1912

Banana Boat, very rare
Marigold	3,000
Blue	2,750

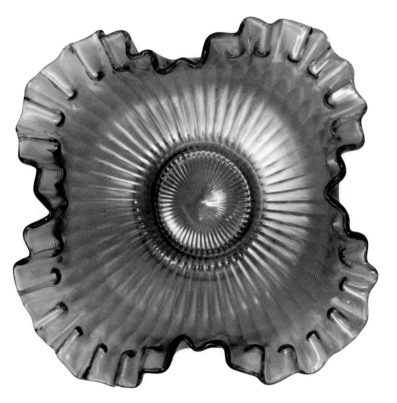

Made by
Fenton, 1911

Bowl, 5" – 6"

Marigold	25
Amethyst or Purple	35
Green	40
Blue	45
Ice Green	55

Bowl, tri-corner, 6½"

Marigold	30
Amethyst or Purple	45
Green	50
Blue	55
Ice Green	70

Bowl, square, 9", scarce

Marigold	70
Green	90

Fern (Fenton)

Made by
Fenton, 1911

Bowl, 7" – 9", rare
Blue   1,100

Made by
Northwood, 1911 – 1912

Compote
Marigold	100
Amethyst or Purple	90
Green	135
Ice Blue*	1,400

*Daisy & Plume exterior

Fern Brand Chocolates

Made by
Northwood, 1912

Plate
Amethyst or Purple   1,300

Made by
U.S. Glass, 1916 – 1917

Bowl, 6" – 10"
Marigold 50
Ice Blue 250

Butter, rare
Marigold 125

Breakfast Set, two-piece, rare
Ice Blue 325

Compote
Marigold 150

Plate, 6", rare
Marigold 200

Plate, 9", rare
Marigold 300

Pitcher, scarce
Marigold 175

Tumbler, scarce
Marigold 45

Sugar, Creamer, or Spooner, rare
Marigold 100

Vase, two sizes
Marigold 250 – 500

File

Also known as
#256

Made by
Imperial, 1909 – 1911

Bowl, 5"
    Marigold   30
    Amethyst or Purple   40

Bowl, 7" – 10"
    Marigold   45
    Amethyst or Purple   50
    Clambroth   60

Compote
    Marigold   40
    Amethyst or Purple   50
    Clambroth   60

Creamer or Spooner
    Marigold   85

Juice Tumbler, rare
    Marigold   300

Lemonade Tumbler Variant, rare
    Marigold   1,000

Pitcher, rare
    Marigold   300
    Amethyst or Purple   500

Tumbler, scarce
    Marigold   100

Sugar
    Marigold   125

Vase Whimsey, from sugar, scarce
    Marigold   350

Also known as
Honeycomb Collar

Made by
Dugan, 1911 – 1912

Bowl, 6" – 8"
Marigold	35
Amethyst or Purple	45
Peach Opalescent	150
White	70

Bride's Basket, complete
Peach Opalescent	150

Plate, 7"
Marigold	50
Amethyst or Purple	200
Peach Opalescent	200
White	200

Plate, Souvenir of Sturgis, Mich.
White	350

Five Hearts

Made by
Dugan?, 1911 – 1912

Bowl, dome base, 8¼"
Marigold	125
Amethyst or Purple	275
Peach Opalescent	300

Bowl, flared, very rare
Marigold	650

Rose Bowl, rare
Marigold	1,300

Made by
Millersburg, 1911

Compote, tall, very rare
Amethyst or Purple   8,500
Green   9,500

Fluffy Peacock

Made by
Fenton, 1911 – 1912

Pitcher

Marigold	325
Amethyst or Purple	700
Green	750
Blue	575

Tumbler

Marigold	40
Amethyst or Purple	70
Green	110
Blue	75

Also known as
Imperial #233

Made by
Imperial, 1909 – 1916

Bowl, 5", scarce
Marigold	65
Amethyst or Purple	95
Clambroth	60

Bowl, 8½", rare
Marigold	150

Forks

Made by
Imperial/Cambridge (crystal), 1910 – 1914?

Cracker Jar, very scarce
Marigold	1,750
Green	600

Also known as
Button and Soda Gold

Made by
Dugan, 1908

Hatpin Holder, very scarce
    Marigold   900
    Amethyst or Purple 1,100

Vase, J.I.P., very scarce
    Marigold   600
    Amethyst or Purple   900

Four Pillars

Made by
Northwood, Dugan (and possibly Millersburg), 1913 – 1917

Vase

Marigold	50
Amethyst or Purple	60
Green	100
Aqua Opalescent	200
Ice Blue	225
Ice Green	250
Sapphire Blue	400

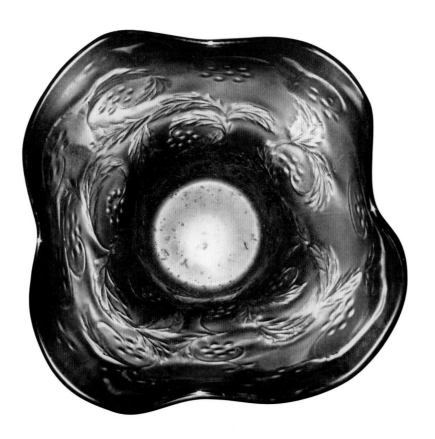

Made by
Fenton, 1911

Hat

Marigold	30
Amethyst or Purple	40
Green	40
Blue	45

Fruit Lustre

Also known as
Late Embossed Fruits (#1914)

Made by
Federal, 1914 – 1923

Tumbler
Marigold   35

Made by
Westmoreland, 1910 – 1913

Punch Bowl and Base, rare

Marigold	600
Amethyst or Purple	700
Peach Opalescent	3,900
Aqua Opalescent	6,000

Punch Cup, rare

Marigold	30
Amethyst or Purple	40
Peach Opalescent	60

Garden Mums

Also known as
Shasta Daisy

Made by
Fenton, 1910

Bowl, 5" – 6", scarce
    Amethyst or Purple   300

Bowl, 5", deep round, rare
    Amethyst or Purple   375

Plate, regular or handgrip, 7", rare
    Amethyst or Purple   450
    Lavender   250

Made by
Dugan, 1912

Bowl, 6" – 7½"
Marigold 35
Amethyst or Purple 110
Peach Opalescent 150
Ice Blue 1,500
White 100

Bowl, 8" – 9½", ruffled
Marigold 75
Amethyst or Purple 600
Peach Opalescent 350
White 350

Bowl, 10", ICS, scarce
Marigold 450
Amethyst or Purple 1,200
Peach Opalescent 950
White 1,000

Compote, rare
Marigold 225
Amethyst or Purple 400
White 500

Plate, 6", rare
Marigold 425
Amethyst or Purple 650
Peach Opalescent 525

Chop Plate, rare
Marigold 4,500
Amethyst or Purple 5,000
Peach Opalescent 7,500

Rose Bowl, rare
Marigold 200

Garden Path Variant

Made by
Dugan, 1912

Bowl, 5¾" – 6½"
Marigold	40
Amethyst or Purple	125
Peach Opalescent	160
Ice Blue	1,300

Bowl, 8" – 10", deep round
Marigold	75
Amethyst or Purple	425
Peach Opalescent	300
White	350

Chop Plate, rare
Marigold	4,500
Amethyst or Purple	5,250
Peach Opalescent	7,250

Chop Plate, Soda Gold exterior
Amethyst or Purple	6,750
Peach Opalescent	7,500

Rose Bowl, rare
Marigold	200

Garland

Made by
Fenton, 1911

Rose Bowl, footed

Marigold	45
Amethyst or Purple	350
Green	400
Blue	90
Amber	425

Made by
Millersburg, 1911

Pitcher, very rare
  Amethyst or Purple 8,500
  Green 9,500

Tumbler, rare
  Marigold 1,000
  Amethyst or Purple 1,150
  Green 1,450

Made by
Fenton, 1911 – 1912

Bowl, scarce
Amethyst or Purple   1,200

Plate, scarce
Amethyst or Purple   1,850

Gevurtz Bros.

Made by
Fenton, 1911 – 1912

Bowl, advertising, scarce
    Amethyst or Purple   800

Plate, advertising, rare
    Amethyst or Purple   2,000

Plate, handgrip, scarce
    Amethyst or Purple   1,400

Also known as
Harvest Time

Made by
U.S. Glass, 1916 – 1917

Reproductions
yes

Decanter with Stopper
Marigold	145
Amethyst or Purple	250

Wine
Marigold	25
Amethyst or Purple	35

Grape Delight

Made by
Dugan/Diamond, 1912

Reproductions
yes

Nut Bowl, footed, 6"
Marigold	50
Amethyst or Purple	120
Blue	80
White	95

Rose Bowl, footed, 6"
Marigold	65
Amethyst or Purple	125
Blue	100
White	65

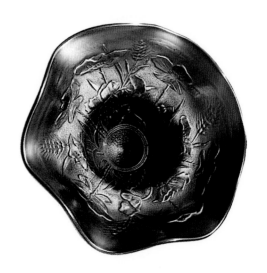

Made by
Northwood, 1914 – 1915

Compote, scarce

Marigold	320
Amethyst or Purple	450
Green	400
Blue	450
Amber	500

Heart and Horseshoe

Made by
Fenton, 1912 – 1913

Bowl, 8½"
    Marigold   2,500

Plate, 9", rare
    Marigold   3,000

Made by
Dugan, 1910

Reproductions
yes

Pitcher
Marigold	250
Amethyst or Purple	1,000
Peach Opalescent	2,500
White	1,100

Tumbler
Marigold	60
Amethyst or Purple	105
White	175
Horehound	125

Tumbler Whimsey
Marigold	350
White	400

Heavy Pineapple

Made by
Fenton, 1916

Bowl, flat or footed, 10"

Marigold	2,800
Blue	3,000
White	2,000
Amber	1,600

Made by
Jeannette, 1927

Tumbler, very rare
Marigold   400

Hobnail Soda Gold

Made by
Imperial, 1914 – 1916

Spittoon, large
Marigold	65
Green	100
Amber	125

Also known as
#282

Made by
Imperial, 1911

Bowl, berry, 5"
Marigold	25
Clambroth	15

Bowl, berry, 10"
Marigold	40
Clambroth	30

Bowl, various shapes, 6" – 12"
Marigold	30
Clambroth	40

Bride's Basket, complete
Marigold	75

Butter
Marigold	80
Amethyst or Purple	195
Green	185
Clambroth	90

Cookie Jar with Lid
Marigold	65
Green	100

Creamer or Spooner
Marigold	45
Amethyst or Purple	85
Green	75
Clambroth	50

Fruit Bowl with Base
Marigold	100
Amethyst or Purple	250
Green	150

Pickle Castor, complete
Marigold	750

Sugar with Lid
Marigold	65
Amethyst or Purple	100
Green	90
Clambroth	60

Vase, flared
Marigold	350
Amethyst or Purple	200

Hobstar and Arches

Also known as
#3027

Made by
Imperial, 1910

Bowl, 9"

Marigold	50
Amethyst or Purple	75
Green	60
Smoke	60

Fruit Bowl with Base

Marigold	125
Amethyst or Purple	300
Green	225

Also known as

Four Fruit and Hobstar

Made by

Westmoreland, 1910

Bowl, 6", rare

Peach Opalescent	115
Aqua Opalescent	300
Marigold Milk Glass	350

Plate, 10½", rare

Ice Blue	385

Hobstar and Tassels

Made by
Imperial, 1909

Bowl, 6", deep round, rare

Marigold	125
Amethyst or Purple	175
Green	225

Bowl, 7" – 8", scarce

Marigold	150
Amethyst or Purple	200
Teal	350

Plate, 7½", rare

Green	900

Also known as
Arched Hobstar

Made by
Possibly U.S. Glass, 1916 – 1917

Bowl, 8" – 10", rare
Marigold   75

Butter, scarce
Marigold   200
Amethyst or Purple   275

Celery, scarce
Marigold   70
Green   275

Compote, scarce
Marigold   90

Pitcher, two shapes, scarce
Marigold   250

Tumbler, two shapes
Marigold   35

Sugar with Lid
Marigold   115

Spooner
Marigold   65

Honeycomb

Made by
Dugan, 1907 (non-carnival), 1910 (carnival)

Rose Bowl
Marigold	90
Peach Opalescent	200

Rose Bowl, pontil base
Marigold	200

Made by
Fenton, 1910 – 1912?

Plate, scarce
    Marigold   225
    Amethyst or Purple 2,850
    Blue   2,100

Indiana Soldiers and Sailors

Made by
Fenton, 1912

Bowl, very rare
Blue   10,000

Plate, very rare
Blue   15,500

Made by
Fenton, 1912 – 1913

Plate, rare
Marigold	16,000
Blue	7,500

Inverted Strawberry

Also known as
Strawberry

Made by
Cambridge, 1915

Reproductions
yes

Bonbon, stemmed with handle, rare
Green 900

Bonbon, Whimsey from Spooner, two-handled, rare
Green 1,700

Bowl, 5"
Marigold 40
Amethyst or Purple 115
Green 75

Bowl, 7½", square, rare
Blue 450

Bowl, 9" – 10½"
Marigold 145
Amethyst or Purple 235
Green 275
Blue 375

Candlesticks, pair, scarce
Marigold 425
Amethyst or Purple 475
Green 950

Celery, very scarce
Amethyst or Purple 600

Green 900
Blue 1,000

Compote, small, very scarce
Marigold 400
Blue 900

Compote, large, very scarce
Marigold 225
Amethyst or Purple 325
Green 450
Blue 1,300

Compote Whimsey, rare
Marigold 1,500

Covered Butter
Marigold 850
Amethyst or Purple 1,100

Creamer, Sugar, or Spooner, each, rare
Marigold 375
Amethyst or Purple 225
Green 325
Blue 425

Hat Whimsey, rare
Blue 950

Ladies' Spittoon, rare
Marigold 900
Amethyst or Purple 1,350
Green 1,200

Milk Pitcher, rare
Amethyst or Purple 5,000

Powder Jar, very scarce
Marigold 200
Green 325

Pitcher, rare
Marigold 2,200
Amethyst or Purple 2,400
Green 2,000

Tumbler, rare
Marigold 135
Amethyst or Purple 165
Green 200
Blue 500

Table Set, two pieces (stemmed), rare
Amethyst or Purple 1,300

Also known as
Thistle

Made by
Cambridge, 1915

Reproductions
yes

Bowl, 5", rare
Amethyst or Purple 150
Green 150

Bowl, 9", rare
Amethyst or Purple 325
Green 325

Bowl Whimsey, footed, rare
Green 600

Butter, rare
Marigold 500
Amethyst or Purple 600
Green 700

Chop Plate, rare
Amethyst or Purple 2,700

Covered Box, rare
Blue 400

Creamer, Sugar, or Spooner, rare
Marigold 350
Amethyst or Purple 400
Green 500

Milk Pitcher, rare
Amethyst or Purple 2,700
Green 2,900

Pitcher, rare
Marigold 3,000
Amethyst or Purple 1,800

Tumbler, rare
Marigold 350
Amethyst or Purple 350

Spittoon, rare
Amethyst or Purple 4,000

Iris

Also known as
Old Fashioned Flag

Made by
Fenton, 1912 – 1913

Buttermilk Goblet

Marigold	25
Amethyst or Purple	65
Green	65
Blue	125
Amber	80

Compote

Marigold	50
Amethyst or Purple	60
Green	60
Blue	90
White	235

Made by
Millersburg?, 1910 – 1911

Bowl, advertising, 6½"
Amethyst or Purple 425

Misspelled version, rare
Amethyst or Purple 1,000

Lacy Dewdrop

Made by
Phoenix, Co-operative Flint, or Westmoreland, 1930s

All pieces are scarce/rare   All items listed are in Pearl Carnival.

Banana Boat
Iridized Moonstone   350

Bowl, covered
Iridized Moonstone   300

Cake Plate
Iridized Moonstone   200

Compote, covered
Iridized Moonstone   450

Goblet
Iridized Moonstone   225

Pitcher
Iridized Moonstone   650

Tumbler
Iridized Moonstone   175

Sugar
Iridized Moonstone   175

Also known as
Lattice and Grapevine, #1563

Made by
Fenton, 1912

Pitcher
Marigold	225
Blue	450
Peach Opalescent	2,200
White	1,600

Tumbler
Marigold	30
Blue	45
Peach Opalescent	500
White	145
Powder Blue	100

Spittoon Whimsey, rare
Marigold	3,500

Leaf and Beads

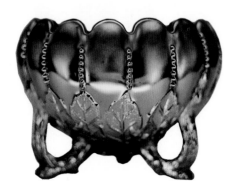

Also known as
Stippled Leaf and Beads

Made by
Northwood, 1906 – 1907

Bowl, dome footed
Marigold	50
Amethyst or Purple	80
Green	70

Candy Dish, three-footed
Marigold	40
Amethyst or Purple	100
Green	85
Blue	325
Aqua Opalescent	700

Nut Bowl, footed, scarce
Marigold	110
Amethyst or Purple	125
Green	85
Blue	300
Aqua Opalescent	1,750
White	325
Lavender	250

Plate Whimsey, rare
Marigold	150
Green	200

Rose Bowl, footed (add 25% for patterned interior)
Marigold	135
Amethyst or Purple	150
Green	165
Blue	225
Aqua Opalescent	350
Ice Blue	1,100
Ice Green	1,450
White	500
Lime Opalescent	2,700

Made by
Millersburg, 1911

Compote, miniature, rare

Marigold	400
Amethyst or Purple	500
Green	525

Leaf Column

Made by
Northwood, 1911 – 1912

Shade
    Amber   100

Vase
Marigold	75
Amethyst or Purple	115
Green	250
Blue	950
Ice Blue	1,400
Ice Green	450
White	325
Lavender	355

Also known as
Stippled Leaf, #1790

Made by
Fenton, 1914

Banana Bowl Whimsey
    Marigold   200

Bowl, footed, 5"
    Marigold   30

Bowl, footed, 10"
    Marigold   60
    Blue   2,000

Butter, footed
    Marigold   175

Creamer, Spooner, footed
    Marigold   75

Plate Whimsey, from Spooner
    Marigold   450

Sugar, footed
    Marigold   90

Pitcher, footed, rare
    Marigold   525
    Blue   725

Tumbler, footed, rare
    Marigold   125
    Blue   165

Lined Lattice

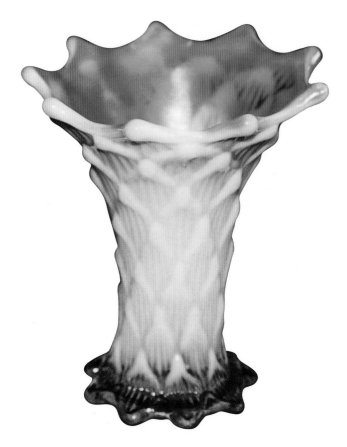

Also known as
Palisades (in opalescent glass)

Made by
Dugan/Diamond, 1912 – 1915

Vase, squat, 5" – 7"		**Vase, 8" – 12"**	
Marigold	225	Marigold	80
Amethyst or Purple	180	Amethyst or Purple	125
Blue	425	Blue	350
Peach Opalescent	300	Peach Opalescent	250
White	200	White	125
Horehound	325	Horehound	275

Also known as
Dancing Daisies

Made by
Northwood, 1914?

Bowl, footed, very rare
Amethyst or Purple   1,800

Little Barrel

Made by
Imperial, 1915 – 1916

One Shape
Marigold	150
Green	200
Smoke	200

Also known as
Sea Lanes, #1604

Made by
Fenton, 1914

Bowl, flat or footed, 5½"

Marigold	95
Amethyst or Purple	145
Blue	150
White	350
Aqua	200

Bowl, flat or footed, 10"

Marigold	175
Amethyst or Purple	425
Blue	425
Ice Green	8,000
White	1,500

Plate, 10½", rare

Marigold	5,000

Long Hobstar

Made by
Imperial, 1910 – 1911

Bowl, 8½"
  Marigold   45

Bowl, 10½"
  Marigold   60

Compote
  Marigold   65

Punch Bowl with Base
  Marigold   125
  Clambroth   150

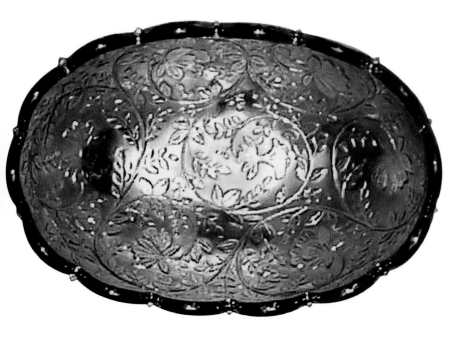

Also known as
Irish Lace

Made by
Westmoreland/Jeannette, 1910 (Westmoreland), 1950 (Jeannette)

Reproductions
yes

Floragold Depression name.
Many shapes and sizes, prices
from $10 – $650, late 1950s.

Lustre Flute

Also known as
Waffle Band

Made by
Northwood, 1909 – 1910

Bonbon
    Amethyst or Purple   50
    Green   50

Bowl, 5½"
    Marigold   25
    Amethyst or Purple   30
    Green   30

Bowl, 8"
    Marigold   50
    Amethyst or Purple   65
    Green   65

Compote
    Amethyst or Purple   55
    Green   50

Creamer or Sugar
    Marigold   40
    Amethyst or Purple   55
    Green   55

Hat
    Marigold   25
    Amethyst or Purple   30
    Green   30

Nappy (from punch cup)
    Marigold   50
    Amethyst or Purple   75
    Green   70

Punch Cup
    Marigold   20
    Amethyst or Purple   25
    Green   20

Sherbet
    Marigold   35

Made by
Diamond, 1924

Bowl, 9", scarce
 Marigold 75
 Amethyst or Purple 150

Plate, 10", rare
 Amethyst or Purple 500
 Amber 400

Rose Bowl, rare
 Marigold 125
 Amethyst or Purple 400

Memphis

Also known as
Northwood's #19

Made by
Northwood, 1910

Berry Bowl, 5"

Marigold	35
Amethyst or Purple	45

Berry Bowl, 10" – 12"

Marigold	125
Amethyst or Purple	350
Aqua Opalescent	5,100

Fruit Bowl with Base

Marigold	325
Amethyst or Purple	400
Green	800
Blue	2,400
Ice Blue	4,000
Ice Green	6,000
White	1,200
Lime Green	2,600

Punch Bowl with Base

Marigold	450
Amethyst or Purple	625
Green	2,300
Ice Blue	4,500
Ice Green	15,000
White	2,100
Lime Green	65

Punch Cup

Marigold	25
Amethyst or Purple	40
Green	50
Ice Blue	85
Ice Green	95

Made by
Fenton, 1912

Compote, large
Marigold	200
Amethyst or Purple	1,350
Green	2,900
Blue	950
White	1,000
Red	9,000
Powder Blue	600

Milady

Also known as
Paneled Bachelor Buttons

Made by
Fenton, 1910

Pitcher		Tumbler	
Marigold	875	Marigold	85
Amethyst or Purple	1,300	Amethyst or Purple	350
Green	1,300	Green	350
Blue	850	Blue	125

Made by
Millersburg, 1911 – 1912

Bowl, 5"
Marigold   40

Bowl, 8½"
Marigold   90
Green   900

Mirrored Lotus

Made by
Fenton, 1912 – 1913

Bowl, 7" – 8½"
Marigold	75
Blue	165
Ice Green	2,500
Celeste Blue	3,000

Plate, 7½", rare
Marigold	500
Blue	650
Celeste Blue	4,900

Rose Bowl, rare
Marigold	325
Blue	500
White	600

Made by
Millersburg, 1911

Pitcher, rare

Marigold	16,500
Amethyst or Purple	13,500
Green	16,000

Tumbler, rare

Marigold	1,000
Amethyst or Purple	2,500
Green	4,000

Multi-Fruits and Flowers

Made by
Millersburg, 1911

Desert, stemmed, rare
    Amethyst or Purple   900
    Green   900

**Punch Bowl with Base,
flared, rare**
    Marigold   1,800
    Amethyst or Purple   2,100
    Green   3,900
    Blue   25,000

**Punch Bowl with Base,
tulip top, rare**
    Marigold   3,800
    Amethyst or Purple   4,300
    Green   4,900
    Blue   55,000

Punch Cup, rare
    Marigold   60
    Amethyst or Purple   85
    Green   100
    Blue   900

Pitcher (either base), rare
    Marigold   4,200
    Amethyst or Purple   8,000
    Green   9,000

Tumbler, rare
    Marigold   900
    Amethyst or Purple   1,000
    Green   1,200

Made by
Millersburg, 1910

Bonbon, rare

Marigold	700
Amethyst or Purple	850
Green	1,400
Olive Green	1,700

Card Tray, rare

Marigold	800
Amethyst or Purple	900
Green	1,200

Nappy, tri-cornered, very rare

Marigold	1,500
Amethyst or Purple	1,200
Green	1,800

Norris N. Smith

Made by
Fenton, 1911 – 1912

Bowl, advertising, scarce
Amethyst or Purple   900

Plate, advertising, 5¾", scarce
Amethyst or Purple   1,800

Made by
Fenton, 1909 – 1912

Bowl, 6"
    Marigold   30

Bowl, 5", ICS, rare
    Marigold   75

Bowl, tri-cornered
    Marigold   40

Card Tray, 6"
    Marigold   40

Plate, 6½", rare
    Marigold   100

Northwood Fine Rib

Made by
Northwood, 1912 – 1915

Vase, 7" – 14"

Marigold	25
Amethyst or Purple	65
Green	45
Blue	165
Ice Blue	180
Ice Green	195
White	100
Horehound	145

Made by
Fenton, 1912

Bowl, scarce
  Amethyst or Purple   1,350

Plate, scarce
  Amethyst or Purple   1,000

Plate, handgrip, scarce
  Amethyst or Purple   1,100

Palm Beach

Made by
U.S. Glass, 1914 – 1916

Banana Bowl

Marigold	100
Amethyst or Purple	175
Honey Amber	175

Bowl, 5" – 6"

Marigold	100
White	95
Honey Amber	90

Bowl, 9"

Marigold	55
White	120
Honey Amber	40

Butter

Marigold	135
White	275
Honey Amber	150

Creamer or Spooner

Marigold	75
White	125
Honey Amber	75

Plate, 9", rare

Marigold	225
Amethyst or Purple	275
White	250

Pitcher

Marigold	325
White	600
Honey Amber	500

Tumbler

Marigold	150
White	140
Honey Amber	100

Rose Bowl Whimsey, rare

Marigold	350
Lime Green	150

Sugar, covered

Marigold	95
Lime Green	125

Vase Whimsey, rare

Marigold	785
Amethyst or Purple	500
White	900

Made by
Northwood, 1909 – 1910

Bonbon, footed
Marigold	60
Amethyst or Purple	90
Green	75

Bowl
Amethyst or Purple	75
Green	70

Creamer or Sugar
Marigold	65

Pitcher, very rare
Amethyst or Purple	22,000

Spooner
Marigold	55

Parlor Panels

Also known as
Lilith

Made by
Imperial, 1909 – 1911

Vase, 4" – 14"
Marigold	110
Amethyst or Purple	325
Green	110
Blue	900
Smoke	725

Also known as
Apple and Pear

Made by
Diamond, 1924 – 1925

Banana Bowl
Marigold	90
Amethyst or Purple	150
Blue	600

Peacock Garden

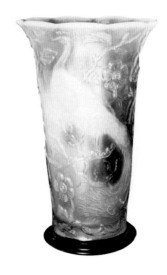

Also known as
Peacock

Made by
Northwood/Fenton, 1913 – Present

Reproductions
yes (Fenton)

Vase, 8", very rare
  Marigold   16,000
  White Opalescent   5,000

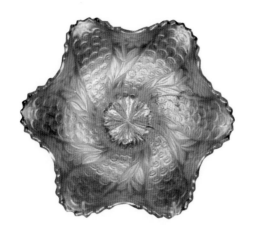

Made by
Westmoreland, 1911

Reproductions
yes

Bowl, very rare
Marigold	1,500
Amethyst or Purple	1,900
Blue Opalescent	2,200

Pebbles

Made by
Fenton, 1912 – 1913

Bowl, sauce
  Marigold   15
  Green   30

Bonbon
  Marigold   25
  Amethyst or Purple 45
  Green   65
  Blue   50

Also known as
Holland Vase

Made by
Millersburg, 1911

Vase, large, either shape, very rare
Marigold	50,000
Amethyst or Purple	50,000
Green	60,000
Blue	65,000

Perfection

Also known as
Beaded Jewel and Leaf

Made by
Millersburg, 1910

Pitcher, rare

Marigold	5,000
Amethyst or Purple	5,500
Green	6,000

Tumbler, rare

Marigold	800
Amethyst or Purple	600
Green	400

Also known as
#682

Made by
Imperial, 1911

Celery Vase
Marigold	60
Amethyst or Purple	90
Smoke	85

Compote
Marigold	50
Black Amethyst	225

Creamer or Sugar
Marigold	35
Smoke	40

Pickle Dish
Marigold	30
Clambroth	35

Rose Bowl
Marigold	65
Smoke	80

Pillar and Sunburst

Also known as
#25194

Made by
Westmoreland, 1910

Bowl, 7½" – 9"
Marigold	45
Amethyst or Purple	50
Peach Opalescent	100
Amber	80

Also known as
Pine Cone Wreath

Made by
Fenton, 1910 – 1912

Bowl, 6"
Marigold	45
Amethyst or Purple	80
Green	150
Blue	65
White	265
Sapphire Blue	200

Bowl, ICS, 6½", scarce
Marigold	75
Amethyst or Purple	100
Green	185
Blue	85

Plate, 6¼"
Marigold	135
Amethyst or Purple	325
Green	375
Blue	250

Plate, 6¼", 12 sided, smooth edge
Blue	350

Plate, 7½"
Marigold	450
Amethyst or Purple	550
Blue	375
Amber	1,000

Pipe Humidor

Made by
Millersburg, 1910

Tobacco Jar with Lid, very rare
Marigold   13,000
Amethyst or Purple   10,000
Green   11,000

Also known as
Two Fruits

Made by
Northwood, 1908 (crystal), 1911 (carnival)

Spooner, rare
Blue   1,800

Sugar, rare
Blue   1,800

Tumbler, very rare
Marigold   2,500
Blue   4,000

Poppy

Made by
Millersburg, 1910

Compote, scarce
Marigold	575
Amethyst or Purple	725
Green	750

Salver, rare
Marigold	2,000
Amethyst or Purple	1,700
Green	1,600

Made by
Fenton, 1915

Bonbon, scarce
    Iridized Custard   1,800

Plate, 7", very rare
    Iridized Custard   8,200

Creamer, very rare
    Iridized Custard   3,500

Premium

Also known as
#635

Made by
Imperial, 1911 – 1914

Candlesticks, pair
Marigold	45
Amethyst or Purple	175
Red	425
Smoke	175

Made by
Imperial, 1910 – 1912

Bowl, 9½", rare
    Marigold   175

Compote
    Marigold   50
    Green   85
    Smoke   80

Vase, stemmed, rare
    Marigold   90

Queen's Lamp

Made by
Unknown, 1909 – 1915

Lamp, complete, rare
Green   3,000

Also known as
Feather and Scroll

Made by
Dugan, 1907 (crystal), 1910 (carnival)

Pitcher, rare
Marigold 900
Amethyst or Purple 2,000

Tumbler, rare
Marigold 200
Amethyst or Purple 250

Ranger

Made by
Imperial (later others in Europe, Mexico, and Australia), 1909

Bowl, round, 4½" – 8"
Marigold   25

Bowl, flared, 6¼" – 10"
Marigold   40
Clambroth   60

Breakfast Set, two pieces
Marigold   90

Cracker Jar
Marigold   80

Nappy
Marigold   45

Pitcher
Marigold   450

Tumbler
Marigold   150

Sherbet, footed
Marigold   55

Vase, 8"
Marigold   95
Clambroth   145

Also known as
Sunshine

Made by
U.S. Glass, 1915?

Bowl, small sauce
Marigold   35

Butter Dish
Marigold   400

Creamer
Marigold   75

Juice Tumbler, rare
Marigold   150

Pitcher, two shapes, very scarce
Marigold   325
Blue   1,400

Pitcher, squat, rare
Marigold   600

Tumbler, scarce
Marigold   135
Blue   350

Sugar
Marigold   95

Tray, rare
Marigold   300
Blue   500

Rococo

Made by
Imperial, 1911

Bowl, 5", footed
Marigold	40
Lavender	275

Bowl, 9", footed, rare
Marigold	175

Vase, 5½"
Marigold	125
Lavender	235

Rose Column

Made by
Millersburg, 1911

Vase, rare

Marigold	5,500
Amethyst or Purple	5,500
Green	3,800
Blue	10,000
Aqua	7,500

Vase, experimental, very rare

Amethyst or Purple	7,500

Roses and Fruit

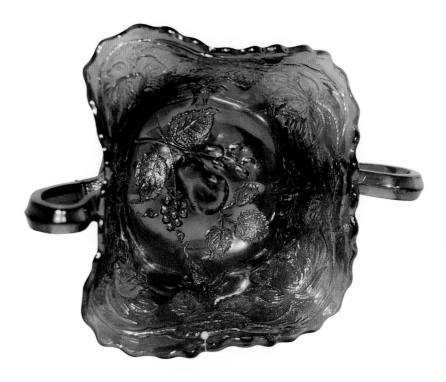

Made by
Millersburg, 1911

Bonbon, footed, rare

Marigold	600
Amethyst or Purple	800
Green	800
Blue	3,000

Made by
Fostoria, 1909 – 1922

Pitcher, very rare
Marigold   900

Tumbler, rare
Marigold   200

Tumbler, advertising, very rare
Marigold   550

Sailboats

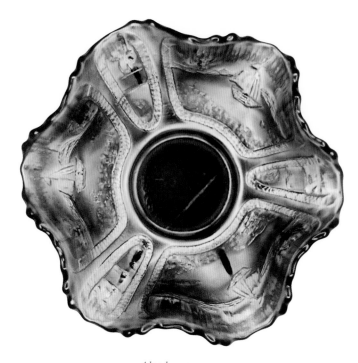

Also known as
Sailboat and Windmill

Made by
Fenton, 1911

Bowl, 6"
Marigold	40
Amethyst or Purple	75
Green	125
Blue	70
Red	600
Aqua	145

Compote
Marigold	65
Blue	195

Goblet
Marigold	225
Amethyst or Purple	400
Green	500
Blue	100
Powder Blue	190

Plate, 6"
Marigold	350
Blue	850
Red	1,000
Lavender	250

Wine
Marigold	35
Blue	80
Vaseline	350

Wine (variant), scarce
Marigold	55
Blue	125

Also known as
Two Band

Made by
Fenton, 1908 – 1924

Bowl, 6"
Marigold	25
Blue	100
White	90
Red	325

Bowl, 8½" – 10", very scarce
Marigold	100
Blue	400
Vaseline	350

Plate, flat, 6½"
Marigold	50
Red	425

Plate, dome base, 7"
Marigold	80
Red	600

Pitcher
Marigold	150
Green	800
Blue	550
Vaseline	350

Tumbler
Marigold	40
Green	225
Blue	300

Seacoast

Also known as
Maine Coast

Made by
Millersburg, 1911

Pin Tray, very scarce
Marigold	1,000
Amethyst or Purple	800
Green	800
Clambroth	900

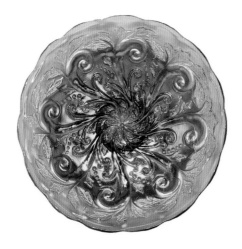

Also known as
Stippled Leaf and Scroll

Made by
Millersburg, 1910

Bowl, 5" – 6½", rare
Marigold	850
Amethyst or Purple	1,000
Green	2,000
Blue	3,000

Bowl, 9", scarce
Marigold	275
Amethyst or Purple	525
Green	400
Blue	2,000

Bowl, ruffled, 10½", scarce
Marigold	400
Amethyst or Purple	600
Green	450
Clambroth	300

Bowl, 6", ICS, very rare
Blue	2,000

Bowl, ice cream, 10½", rare
Marigold	500
Amethyst or Purple	1,600
Green	1,900
Blue	5,500

Plate, 10", rare
Marigold	1,800
Amethyst or Purple	2,500
Green	3,350

Shell and Jewel

Also known as
Westmoreland, 1909 – 1912

Reproductions
yes

Creamer with Lid
Marigold	55
Amethyst or Purple	65
Green	60
White	90

Sugar with Lid
Marigold	55
Amethyst or Purple	65
Green	60
White	90

Sugar Whimsey
Green	200

Made by
Dugan, 1910 – 1911

Banana Bowl, 9½", rare
    Peach Opalescent   375

Basket Whimsey, handled, rare
    Marigold   225
    Peach Opalescent   350

Bowl, 8"
    Marigold   35
    Amethyst or Purple   45
    Green   125
    Peach Opalescent   140

Bowl, 9" (Lily of the Valley decoration)
    Peach Opalescent   100

Hat
    Marigold   30
    Amethyst or Purple   45
    Green   65

Smooth Panels

Made by
Imperial, 1915

Bowl, 6½"
    Marigold   30
    Smoke   35

Rose Bowl, scarce
    Marigold   50
    Smoke   75

Sweet Pea Vase, scarce
    Marigold   75
    White   100
    Clambroth   60

Vase, squat, 4" – 7"
    Marigold   50
    Red   250
    Marigold Milk Glass   300

Vase, standard, 8" – 14"
    Marigold   40
    Amethyst or Purple   150
    Green   175
    Red   325
    Marigold Milk Glass   250

Vase, funeral, 15" – 18"
    Marigold   125
    Red   800
    Teal   350

Made by
Westmoreland, 1910

Bowl, flat, 6" – 9"
Marigold	40
Amethyst or Purple	55
Green	50
Peach Opalescent	75
Blue Opalescent	125
Teal	75

Bowl, dome base, 5" – 7½"
Green	60
Peach Opalescent	85
Blue Opalescent	125
Teal	75

Compote
Marigold	35
Amethyst or Purple	45
Green	55
Amber	75

Plate, 7" – 9"
Marigold	75
Amethyst or Purple	100
Green	110
Amber	150

Rose Bowl
Marigold	40
Amethyst or Purple	70
Amber	85

Soda Gold

Also known as
Soda Gold and Spider Web

Made by
Imperial (Dugan also made a version), 1911

Bowl, 9"
    Marigold   45
    Smoke   55

Candlesticks, 3½", each
    Marigold   55
    Smoke   60

Chop Plate, scarce
    Marigold   125

Pitcher
    Marigold   200
    Smoke   350

Tumbler
    Marigold   50
    Smoke   200

Shakers, scarce
    Marigold   125
    Smoke   140

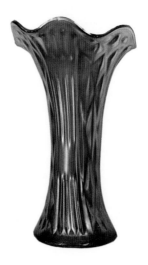

Also known as
#916

Made by
Fenton, 1909 – 1912

Vase, 8" – 15"
Marigold	70
Amethyst or Purple	135
Green	140
Blue	95

Spector's Department Store

Also known as
Heart & Vine

Made by
Fenton, 1910 – 1912

Plate, advertising (Spector's), rare
Marigold   1,600

Also known as
#1028

Made by
Dugan/Diamond, 1910 – 1920s

Vase, 8" – 13"

Marigold	35
Amethyst or Purple	75
Blue	150
Peach Opalescent	75
White	85

Starfish

Also known as
Stippled Starfish Medallion

Made by
Dugan, 1911

Bonbon, handled, scarce

Amethyst or Purple	200
Peach Opalescent	165
White	325

Compote

Marigold	45
Amethyst or Purple	185
Green	75
Peach Opalescent	125

Made by
Fenton, 1911

Pitcher, rare
Marigold	6,500
Blue	3,500
White	18,000

Star Medallion

Also known as
Imperial #671

Made by
Imperial, 1911 – 1920

Bowl, 5" – 5½", dome footed
Marigold 25
White 50

Bowl, 7" – 9"
Marigold 30
Smoke 40

Bowl, square, 7"
Marigold 40
Smoke 45

Butter
Marigold 100

Celery Tray
Marigold 60
Clambroth 50

Compote
Marigold 45

Creamer, Spooner, Sugar, each
Marigold 60

Custard Cup
Marigold 20

Goblet
Marigold 45
Smoke 60

Handled Celery
Marigold 80
Smoke 65

Ice Cream, stemmed, small
Marigold 35

Milk Pitcher
Marigold 80
Green 95
Smoke 80

Tumbler, two sizes
Marigold 30
Green 50
Clambroth 50

Pickle Dish
Marigold 40

Plate, 5"
Marigold 50
Clambroth 35

Plate, 10"
Marigold 70
Clambroth 85

Vase, 6"
Marigold 40
Clambroth 45

Star of David and Bows

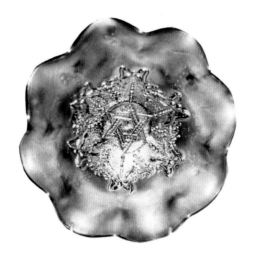

Also known as
Star of David Medallion

Made by
Northwood, 1910

Bowl, 8½"

Marigold	50
Amethyst or Purple	175
Green	125
Amber	200

Star Spray

Made by
Imperial, 1910 – 1912

Bowl, 7"
Marigold   35
Smoke   40

Bride's Basket, complete, rare
Marigold   90
Smoke   125

Plate, 7½", scarce
Marigold   75
Smoke   95

Made by
Millersburg, 1912

Card Tray Whimsey, two-handled, very rare
Amethyst or Purple   2,400

Nappy, two-handled, very rare
Amethyst or Purple   2,200
Green   2,300
Vaseline   2,600

Stippled Estate

Made by
Dugan/Model Flint, 1909

Bud Vase
Marigold	150
Peach Opalescent	200
Ice Green	225

Also known as
Stippled Cosmos

Made by
Dugan, 1910 – 1911

**Bowl, 8½" (add 25% for Lily
of the Valley decoration)**
Peach Opalescent   85

Stippled Strawberry

Also known as
Strawberry

Made by
U.S. Glass, 1928 – 1931

Pitcher, rare
Marigold   350

Sherbet, stemmed
Marigold   60

Tumbler
Marigold   95

Made by
Belmont, 1920s

Child's Plate, 7½"
Marigold   75

Stream of Hearts

Made by
Fenton, 1910 – 1912

Compote, rare
    Marigold   150

Goblet, rare
    Marigold   225

Made by
Westmoreland, 1909 – 1911

Reproductions
yes

Creamer or Sugar with Lid
    Amethyst or Purple   100
    Green   100

Rose Bowl Whimsey
    Green   150
    Black Amethyst   175

Sunflower Pin Tray

Made by
Millersburg, 1910 – 1911

Reproductions
yes

Pin Tray, scarce
Marigold	800
Amethyst or Purple	600
Green	625

Made by
Northwood, 1910 – 1911

Pitcher
    Marigold   165

Tumbler
    Marigold   70
    Amethyst or Purple   75

Thin and Wide Rib

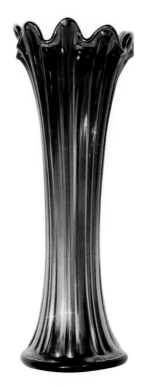

Also known as
Thin Rib

Made by
Northwood, 1910

Vase, ruffled
Marigold	35
Amethyst or Purple	60
Green	60
Blue	125
Ice Blue	275
Ice Green	300
Ice Lavender	600

Vase, J.I.P. shape
Marigold	85
Amethyst or Purple	175
Green	175
Blue	240
Teal	250

Made by
Imperial, 1912 – 1914

Vase, 5½", rare
　　Marigold　　　　　　400
　　Amethyst or Purple　1,700

Tobacco Leaf

Made by
Westmoreland, 1909 (Possibly U.S. Glass)

Champagne
Clear   100

Made by
Dugan, 1911

Bowl, 6" – 8"
Marigold	25
Amethyst or Purple	30
Green	65
Peach Opalescent	75
Vaseline	125

Hat
Marigold	30
Amethyst or Purple	40
Green	70

Tulip

Made by
Millersburg, 1911

Compote, 9", rare
Marigold	1,600
Amethyst or Purple	1,500
Green	1,800

Made by
Millersburg, 1911

Vase, 6" – 12", rare
Marigold   550
Amethyst or Purple   750
Green   850

Twisted Rib

Also known as
#1016

Made by
Dugan, 1912 – 1918

Vase, various sizes

Marigold	35
Amethyst or Purple	75
Blue	150
Peach Opalescent	75
White	85

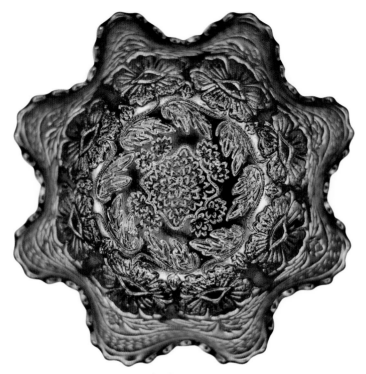

Also known as
Dogwood and Marsh Lily

Made by
Fenton, 1915

Bowl, footed, 6" – 7"
Marigold	25
Amethyst or Purple	60
Green	65
Blue	55

Bowl, footed, 8" – 10"
Marigold	75
Amethyst or Purple	400
Green	250
Blue	375
Red	5,500
Smoke	1,650

Bowl, spatula footed, 8"
Marigold	90
Amethyst or Purple	110
Green	140
Blue	110
Red	1,800
Vaseline	135

Bowl, 8" – 9", flat, rare
Marigold	150

Plate, footed, 9"
Marigold	700
Green	675
Blue	650

Plate, 13", rare
Marigold	2,900

Rose Bowl, rare
Marigold	125
Amethyst or Purple	150
Green	450
Blue	175
White	375
Red	4,500
Smoke	500

Rose Bowl, giant, rare
Marigold	250
Blue	800

Valentine

Also known as
#14

Made by
Northwood, 1907 (crystal), 1909 (carnival)

Bowl, 5", scarce
Marigold	100
Amethyst or Purple	225

Bowl, 10", scarce
Marigold	400

Also known as
Kenneth

Made by
Ohio Flint (crystal), 1907; Millersburg (carnival), 1912

Bowl, 10½", rare
Marigold   500

Butter, rare
Marigold   950

Creamer, rare
Marigold   500

Sugar, rare
Marigold   625

Vase (lamp base), 9¼", rare
Marigold   1,000
Green   1,400

Victorian

Made by
Dugan, 1912

Bowl, 10" – 12", rare
Amethyst or Purple   350
Peach Opalescent   2,500

Bowl, ICS, rare
Amethyst or Purple   1,000

Also known as
Banded Portland

Made by
U.S. Glass, 1901 (crystal), 1912 – 1915 (carnival)

Puff Jar
    Marigold   125

Toothpick
    Marigold   150

Tumbler
    Marigold   150

Waffle

Made by
U.S. Glass, 1920s

Open Sugar or Creamer
Marigold   65

Also known as
#698

Made by
Imperial, 1910 – 1912

Reproductions
yes

Basket, handled, 10"
Marigold	50
Teal	175

Bowl, 7" – 9"
Marigold	30

Bowl, 8", square
Marigold	45

Bowl, 11½"
Marigold	55
Clambroth	65

Butter
Marigold	100

Creamer
Marigold	60

Nappy
Marigold	40

Parfait Glass, stemmed
Marigold	30
Clambroth	35

Pitcher
Marigold	125
Clambroth	150

Punch Bowl and Base
Marigold	110
Clambroth	165

Tumbler, scarce
Marigold	275
Clambroth	350

Tumbler Variant, rare
Clambroth	500

Plate, 6"
Marigold	30
Clambroth	40

Plate, 10" – 12", any shape
Marigold	90
Clambroth	150

Punch Bowl
Marigold	175
Teal	250

Punch Cup
Marigold	20
Teal	35

Rose Bowl
Marigold	75

Shakers, pair
Marigold	75

Sherbet
Clambroth	35

Spittoon, scarce
Marigold	75
Clambroth	85

Sugar
Marigold	60

Vase, 8" – 11"
Marigold	40
Clambroth	55

Washboard

Also known as
Diamond and Fan

Made by
Not confirmed, 1930 – 1960

Butter
    Marigold   70

Creamer, 5½"
    Marigold   45

Punch Cup
    Marigold   15

Tumbler
    Marigold   85

Made by
Northwood, 1911

Bowl with Lid, very rare
Amethyst or Purple   8,000

Sherbet, very rare
Amethyst or Purple   6,000

Sweetmeat with Lid, very rare
Amethyst or Purple   8,000
Green   9,500

Wildflower (Millersburg)

Made by
Millersburg, 1911

Compote, jelly, rare
    Marigold   1,300
    Amethyst or Purple 1,700

Compote, ruffled, rare
    Marigold   900
    Amethyst or Purple 1,300
    Green   1,800

Wildflower (Northwood)

Made by
Northwood, 1905 (crystal), 1909 – 1910 (carnival)

Compote (plain interior)
Marigold	250
Amethyst or Purple	300
Green	300
Blue	425

Wild Rose (Millersburg)

Also known as
Lucille

Made by
Riverside, 1907 (crystal); Millersburg, 1911 (crystal and carnival)

Lamp, small, rare
Marigold	1,000
Amethyst or Purple	1,200
Green	1,100

Lamp, medium, rare
Marigold	1,200
Amethyst or Purple	1,500
Green	1,300

Medallion Lamp, rare
Marigold	2,400
Amethyst or Purple	2,400
Green	2,400

Lamp, marked Riverside, very rare
Green	3,000

Wild Rose (Northwood)

Also known as
Shell and Wild Rose

Made by
Northwood, 1905 (opalescent), 1909 (carnival)

Bowl, footed, open edge, 6"

Marigold	75
Amethyst or Purple	120
Green	100
Blue	300
Horehound	300

Wisteria

Also known as
Wisteria and Lattice

Made by
Northwood, 1912 – 1914

Bank Whimsey, rare
White   3,500

Pitcher, rare
Ice Blue   13,000
White   4,700

Tumbler, rare
Ice Blue   600
Ice Green   525
White   450

Vase Whimsey, very rare
Green   17,000

Woodpecker and Ivy

Made by
Millersburg, 1912

Vase, very rare
Marigold	4,500
Green	6,000
Vaseline	7,500

Zig Zag

Made by
Millersburg, 1912

Bowl, round or ruffled, 9½"
Marigold	300
Amethyst or Purple	400
Green	450

Bowl, square, 8½" – 9½"
Marigold	550
Amethyst or Purple	800
Green	950
Clambroth	500

Sauce Bowl, square, 6", very rare
Marigold	2,000

Bowl, tri-cornered, 10"
Marigold	500
Amethyst or Purple	750
Green	900

Bowl, tri-cornered, 6½", very rare
Marigold	2,000

Card Tray, rare
Green	1,100

Other Titles by Bill Edwards & Mike Carwile

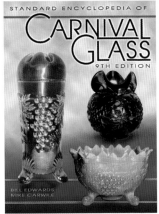

Standard Encyclopedia of Carnival Glass, Ninth Edition

One of our more popular titles, this ninth edition introduces almost 200 new patterns and over 300 new photographs, many never before printed, bringing this edition's total to over 2,000 color patterns. All pieces and patterns are described in detail with important facts, colors, histories, and sizes. The bound-in price guide also includes virtually every piece of carnival glass ever made with prices given for each color in each pattern. We consider this edition the best one yet, and we know it will continue to command the respect of glass collectors worldwide.

8½ x 11, 432 Pgs., $29.95

Standard Encyclopedia of Opalescent Glass, Fifth Edition

Glass production by both American and English glass companies from 1880 to 1930 is covered in this volume. With around 130 new patterns featured, this expanded volume now holds over 850 color photographs. Detailed information on several prominent glass manufacturers is again included, and the attached price guide has been enlarged to include nearly 6,400 pieces in six different colors. A new feature of the price guide is the addition of values for the "after 1930" section of the book, not priced in previous editions. *Standard Encyclopedia of Opalescent Glass, Fifth Edition*, is sure to shine on your bookshelf.

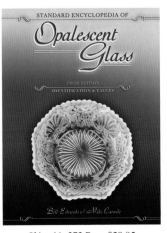

8½ x 11, 272 Pgs., $29.95

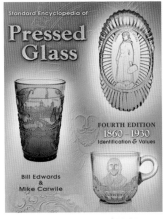

8½ x 11, 384 Pgs., $29.95

Standard Encyclopedia of Pressed Glass, Fourth Edition

American pressed glass, which was at its zenith in the 1870s, entails hundreds of patterns and dozens of shapes with elaborate geometric, animal, fruit, and floral designs. This all-new collector's encyclopedia features over 200 new patterns and photographs, bringing the total to more than 1,500 photos showcasing the exquisite patterns and beautiful colors of the quality pressed glass produced for 60 years in America. This encyclopedia is not only aesthetically pleasing, but also historically correct. Collectors are sure to be pleased with *Standard Encyclopedia of Pressed Glass, Fourth Edition*.

Schroeder's ANTIQUES Price Guide

Schroeder's ANTIQUES Price Guide

Twenty-third Edition

OUR #1 BEST-SELLER! 2005

Identification & Values of Over 50,000 Antiques & Coll...

8½" x 11" • 608 pages • $14.95

OUR #1 BEST-SELLER!

...is the
#1 bestselling
antiques & collectibles
value guide
on the market today,
and here's why...

• More than 400 advisors, well-
known dealers, and top-notch
collectors work together with our
editors to bring you accurate
information regarding pricing
and identification.

• More than 50,000
items in over 500 cate-
gories are listed along
with hundreds of sharp
original photos that illus-
trate not only the rare and
unusual, but the common,
popular collectibles as well.

• Each large close-up shot shows important details
clearly. Every subject is represented with histories
and background information, a feature not found
in any of our competitors' publications.

• Our editors keep abreast of newly developing trends,
often adding several new categories a year as the need
arises.

Without doubt, you'll find
*Schroeder's Antiques
Price Guide*
the only one to buy for reliable
information and values.

COLLECTOR BOOKS
P.O. Box 3009
Paducah, KY 42002–3009
www.collectorbooks.com